Waiting for the
Small Ship of Desire

Poems by Allan Cooper

POTTERSFIELD PRESS
Lawrencetown Beach, Nova Scotia, Canada

Library and Archives Canada Cataloguing in Publication

Title: Waiting for the small ship of desire / poems by Allan Cooper.

Names: Cooper, Allan, 1954- author.

Description: Poems.

Identifiers: Canadiana (print) 20200172751 | Canadiana (ebook) 20200172794 | ISBN 9781989725016

(softcover) | ISBN 9781989725023 (HTML)

Classification: LCC PS8555.O587 W35 2020 | DDC C811/.54—dc23

Cover image and author photograph: Copyright © Laurie Armstrong Cooper, 2020

Cover design by Gail LeBlanc

Pottersfield Press gratefully acknowledges the financial support of the Government of Canada for our publishing activities. We also acknowledge the support of the Canada Council for the Arts and the Province of Nova Scotia which has assisted us to develop and promote our creative industries for the benefit of all Nova Scotians.

Pottersfield Press
248 Leslie Road
East Lawrencetown, Nova Scotia, Canada, B2Z 1T4
Website: www.PottersfieldPress.com
To order, phone 1-800-NIMBUS9 (1-800-646-2879) www.nimbus.ns.ca

Printed in Canada

Pottersfield Press is committed to preserving the environment and the appropriate harvesting of trees and has printed this book on Forest Stewardship Council® certified paper.

Conseil des arts du Canada Canada Council for the Arts

Funded by the Government of Canada Financé par le gouvernement du Canada

Canadä

Arts Nova Scotia Nouvelle-Écosse NOVA SCOTIA

MIX
Paper from responsible sources
FSC
www.fsc.org FSC® C103567

For Laurie

with love

The three thousand worlds
are inside this plum blossom;
the scent is God.

– Shinkichi Takahashi

TABLE OF CONTENTS

IV   *Broken Psalms*

I

The Small Ship

THE SHELL

Everything's turning,
even the grass.
Its darkened blades
are the gold we longed for all summer.

~~

The love we carry
is enough.
It fills the ripened apples
and knocks them to the ground.

~~

Give me the light inside the shell
turning in the tumbling tides.
I'll ride that small ship
beyond the shores of sorrow and loss.

TWO GLIMPSES

I *The Toad*

Here at my feet in last year's grass a toad has
hunkered down from the wind. When I touch his pebbly
back, he hunches down even further in the tawny grass.
I can just see his white throat moving in and out, slow as
the pulse of the universe. He is unassuming, practical, a
small bag of stones left out in the sun to dry.

II *A Porcupine*

When a porcupine wanders out of the goldenrod,
what should we expect? One or two quills left behind,
firm and slender and black. Look how the ink rises in the
quill! We'll have to pay a lot for these gifts.

THE WINTER WASP

We love the smallest things –
the wasp that wakes
and flutters on the floor
as if spring were rising
from the earth again.
What is it that shakes us,
shocks every cell of our bodies?
My friends, there are things
we may never know.
But what we love
is enough to wake the world.

READING OLAV H. HAUGE IN WINTER

Reading your poems
is like trying on someone else's coat:
a wool coat, black and coarse,
practical as a chunk of firewood.
This afternoon thirty robins
landed in the mountain ash.
You would have loved that,
and the wild dance
as they flapped against the window,
drunk on fermented berries.

ALL DAY

All day I've been nurturing something
inside me: the oak leaf frozen on the snow,
the teeth of the field mouse stained brown
by tiny seeds.

DECEMBER

The little ones are out there gathering.
The last light catches in their wings
as they disappear among the dark spruce boughs.

BIRDSONG, DUSK

What if I lost everything
but my love for the world?
What if I lost everything
but my love for you?
Look how swiftly
the chickadees
fly in and out
of the feeder. My love
for you and for the world
is like that.

THE WILD

The wild misses us.
A cricket sings from inside a shoe.
A spider spins her web from shirt to shirt to shirt.
I dreamed a sparrow sang outside my door.
And you were there.

THE PERFECT SILENCE

— three poems after Yuan Mei

I've spent a month in solitude, alone at my desk.
All the books I'd forgotten are clear to me again.
Poems gather like water in the deepest pools,
rising from the perfect silence of the world.

~~

The last apricot blossoms are fading; rain falls, almost in
    silence.
The green of the moss rises and enters my clothes.
Sudden wind blows through the window,
scattering blossoms and poems across the room!

~~

It seems as if I'm folded in by thousands
of mountains, nowhere to go.
Until you finally arrive there's no path that leads here.
And once you get here, there's nowhere else to go.

THREE AUTUMN POEMS FOR YUAN MEI

A smoky light rises from the anthill.
There are green men travelling in the seeds of wild grass.
I stand beneath a spruce dead two years, tall and silver.
The dark hollow at its base knows the grief of earth.

~~

The red of sunset catches in a fallen branch.
The moss is slow, huddled close to earth.
I walk alone, and feel the silence
rising from the colours of the mountain rocks.

~~

Today I want one or two things only:
the vole poking his nose from his mossy grotto,
the brown and purple light
reflected on the beetle's back.

THE WINTER OAK

What would it be like
if we really saw each other?
Would that energy overwhelm us,
or as Marina Tsvetaeva said to Rilke
would we be completely healed,
completely whole, like light
moving through apple blossoms in spring?

Would we come to a place where language
ends and becomes birdsong? Would it be
like seeing a cell dividing,
the glow of the body of someone in love,
like putting our ear to the trunk of an oak
and hearing for the first time
the rings beginning to grow?

Ring after ring, all of our losses and grief
transformed into light and healing power –
for the only way we can move forward
is like this. Part of us is already home,
like the winter oak, the bare branches
clear against the sky, no longer caring
if the darkness continues to fall.

DAISY AND SPARROWS

Tiny blossom, swaying in heavy wind, your tough roots gripping the coral wall. Your centre is one ray of light; your petals the elegant feathers of an unnamed bird. Where have you gone? What kind of love is this that disappears so suddenly? Oh there you are, facing the wind, hanging on for life, for dear life.

~~

Have you seen the fox sparrows lighting down in the grass? There are things I have to do, and despite this crazy wind I will do them, one by one, until the wind settles down for a while, and the light comes out, and the fox sparrows find a little opening in the grass. All I want to do is live. Despite myself, the wind is settling down in the tawny grass.

II

The Red Peony

In memory of my mother

A MAPLE BRANCH

I find the branch of a maple, about two feet long, lying among the moss. At first it resembles a branch that has died and broken off in the winter winds. But the end still has some green to it, hazy and light. Bits of lichen adhere to it, some a deep rusty red, others the hanging light green shreds of old man's beard. There are spiky pieces at the ends of the twigs that arch like the branches of river willows. This is where the seed pods were attached, and where new blossoms might have opened in the spring.

When my mother was dying, she resembled an ancient fetus. Her eyes, a milky white, sometimes opened and looked straight up. A few times she would hear my voice and turn toward me. It was as if she was in some watery element that none of us know of yet.

I told her I was writing this book for her, that it was hers, that she had taught me all the compassion and love that I would need to carry me through this world. I said, "I love you very much." She opened her eyes for the first time in hours, craned her head toward me, and whispered in a voice almost gone, "I love you."

Six months later I stand in the chill of April, wondering what to do, what to say – part of me torn away, another adrift in the placenta of memory.

THE DREAM OF CHANGES

In the dream I'm standing near the entryway of
my mother's ancestral house. It seems familiar, and yet
something has changed. She and I are the only people in
the dream; in fact we're the only people left in the world.
The foundation of the house is hewn fieldstone, covered
in moss. A small spring-fed stream flows beside it.

The entryway leads to a French door, which my
mother opens. The room is black inside, cavernous,
a storehouse for grief and pain. I understand that if I
dropped a pebble into the blackness it would fall and fall
and never reach the bottom. My mother says, "This is
where God goes to mull over the darkness of the world."

I find a small bottle of open wine in a rack, and
old letters and cards with primitive drawings of birds and
animals. I pour a libation of wine on the earthen floor.
My mother says in a slow clear voice, "If you want to
make any changes, you should do it now."

THE WHITE FENCE

This white fence says
there are now two worlds between us.
And while I can't cross over
I will walk around the fence to meet you.

DEER TRACKS AT DUSK

Tonight, at dusk, the sky was pink, azure, and orange.
Deer tracks wandered around the house
as we sometimes wander, in joy or grief,
held inside some moment
that won't let us go. So we wander, walking off the joy
or pain as if too much of either
is more than we can bear.

Perfect tracks across the centre
of your grave!
Enough to make me believe that the things of this world
know something about our loss.
There's a path that moves through us
and around us. We follow it,
even when we don't know where we're going.

TWO WEEKS

I woke from the dream in the middle of the night, almost two weeks to the minute after you'd died. My wife and daughter were waiting at the open door of your old bedroom. There were two bookcases at the back of the room where the headboard of your bed used to be.

You stood in the middle of the room. First you beckoned Katie in, and bent down and hugged her and kissed her. Then you gestured to Laurie, and held her and kissed her. Then they left the room. You called me in with your hand, but I wasn't to touch you – it seemed the bond between us was too strong, and you were protecting me from being drawn into the other world. You walked to the bookcases, lined with so many of your books, then turned around and looked me straight in the eye. You raised your hands and face. "My spirit went straight up," you said.

NIGHT DREAM VOICE

If you hear someone,
stop, listen.
Talk to them.
There are angels everywhere.
They're moving through us all the time.

THE BOOK OF ROSES

In the dream I walked the back road just before
the first light broke above the hills. I was looking for
something – I don't remember what – when I saw the
branch of an immense rose bush hanging over the centre
of the road. At the end of the branch one red blossom,
almost ready to open, hung heavily toward the ground.
The blossom was as large as a three-gallon pail.

Red petals the size of dinner plates were scattered in
the dirt at the side of the road. I thought, *I should gather
these for my daughter*. I saw Katie in a room sitting at a
table, working intently, sorting the petals, writing a book
called *The Secret Book of Roses*.

A car drove by quickly, but the rose remained intact.
Not one petal stirred or was damaged. Something told me
not to touch the rose or the petals. There was no scent
that I could discern. But the rose moved inside me like
a pendulum, swaying in the moist air, rocking back and
forth like a woman rocking a child, her tear-shaped petals
fallen to the earth.

THE RED PEONY

– after a watercolour by Albrecht Dürer

The red peony is a woman who tends her garden
alone, her red cap pulled down over her face. We don't
know who she is. All we know is she seems to be listening
for a sound which is coming, a sound not ominous or
loud, but which is felt by a body aging as the earth ages.
And the one unopened blossom lifted toward the sky is
the part of us that wants to live forever.

III

The Star's Way Home

THE STAR'S WAY

Yes, the stars know their way home
as we drift toward equinox
and those moist spring nights
I loved as a boy – nights I carried inside me
like a worn notebook, the corners bent
but full of praise words, healing words.

There are men who believe
that all words must be sober,
exact as a surgeon's knife, no snails
glistening through the grass, no
mystery of the cricket singing,
hidden near cool roots.

James Wright invited the insects
to join him, and Robert loves
four pigeon grass heads,
scarce and fine. Poetry
is a kind of desire, something
we long to hold but will never own.

Right now I'm waiting for the gold
of the day to touch
my shoulder. I'm waiting
for the dusk to come, the crows
flying home, the black rags of their voices rising
inside my chest.

THE RING

When despair comes to me, that troubled friend,
sometimes for days on end, I put on my father's old
shirt, or make soup with my grandmother's spoon, or
remember the invisible child who came to me when I was
four. He stayed with me for months. One day he had to
leave, and he gave me a silver ring. Father, grandmother,
spirit child lost to everyone but me, when I remember
you the day shines, and fills with the coins of love.

POEM FOR RETA

Just now, sitting alone,
I remembered my grandmother
holding me in her arms.
Isn't it bittersweet
when they come back to us
and we feel their warmth,
that comfort, that home?

Doesn't it seem sometimes
that the whole world wants to join us,
the hummingbird that hovered
six inches from our face,
the orange cat who brought
her sister and two kittens to the door
and decided to stay?

There are sunsets that let their rose and gold
linger far into the dusk. Words
come to us, soft clear voices:
all the men and women we've known
whose trust and care
increase the way
we love this world.

THE PIANO

My grandfather had elegant hands.
At Christmas he played the piano,
and it was always his timing
that caught me, each note
as precise
as the hands of a New Haven clock.

Each Sunday morning
my father played the tenor parts
of an anthem with his left hand,
playing them
over and over again
before he went to church.

And it's only right
that my mother should enter this poem.
She's playing "Yellow Submarine"
and singing with gusto. I'm playing
my father's clarinet. And all the oceans
of the world are moving beneath us.

YUAN MEI

Over two hundred years ago, in his old age,
Yuan Mei wrote a poem called "Planting Trees":

I'm an old man planting trees,
but don't laugh neighbours.
We all know that death is coming
but it's best not to worry about it all the time.

It's good to leave young trees
behind you, rows and rows
leading off into a distance
that diminishes to a single point
like a period at the end of a sentence.
Yuan Mei would have liked
the dozen red spruce growing on the side hill
behind my house; they've been there
for one hundred and fifty years – old oxygen makers,
sifters of dirt and stone, messengers sending
information back and forth to each other
through their roots, their crowns, year after year –

nest providers
for the birds of heaven.

THE TEACHER

– in memory of Robert Calvert

Yesterday I felt a sudden love for an old teacher I
hadn't seen in many years. He stood with two canes, his
white hair and beard as wild as William Blake's Jehovah.
We talked – his wife dead ten years, his father one
hundred years old – and the years unravelled in the wind.
How many old fathers do we carry inside us? Surely
I would carry this man down to the River Styx, place
two coins, grieve again for what the world has lost and
forgotten. I would tell Charon, "No matter what, take
care of this man," as the boat slides silently across the
unknown waters.

YELLOW TRANSPARENTS

Each year
it happens again:
apples
from a hidden tree
appear in the brook.

Slowly, they're
nudged along
by the current
until they find
their way

out to the bay.
Does
this matter?
And what carries you
when you fall?

THE WATERS OF THIS WORLD

I bought the galvanized pail
at the Dollar store
for three dollars
and twenty-five cents.
The pail
is sturdy and light,
with a wood and wire handle
made for easy lifting.
Three gallons of water,
no more, no less,
filled to the brim.
I use the pail to add
cold spring water
to freshen the wash,
not because I have to,
but because my grandmother
did before me,
and her mother before her,
and a great-great-aunt before her.

~

The pail was made in China.
The inside was etched when the steel
was rolled out flat. The markings
resemble the leaves
of the sweet white clover.

The empty pail makes a hollow ringing sound
when I put it down: last call, last
dirge for the dying and the lost,
a lilt or cadence in a voice
we haven't heard in years.

~

It's water that freshens the world,
bedrock water that's been flowing
beneath the earth
for hundreds of years.
It spills out now,

part of the light and promise of the day.

A POEM ABOUT SADNESS

I've carried this sadness with me
most of my life. I felt it first
when I was a young boy,
standing near a deer enclosure
at the end of a long path
in the brown of bleak autumn –
the brown backs of deer,
the brown sadness I carried
in my shoulders
and my childlike heart.
                          I felt it again
when my grandfather died.
I was ten. The sadness
overwhelmed me, so they gave me
a small yellow pill
that made me feel like
I was in a coma
for five years. *Where*
did he go? How
can I find him?
These questions slowly
disappeared until I found
my life stretching out
before me again.
                          What
do I gain from
this sadness? I wear its weight
like a heavy black coat,
a sackcloth filling with rain.
Can I let it go? Somewhere
water is shining,
in spite of our sadness,
in spite of our loss. I think
I'll go find it.

A POEM ABOUT HORSES

My grandfather was wild when he was young.
His brother Claude had a team of horses.
One evening my grandfather
hitched the team to a wagon
and drove them through Alma West,
down Church Hill, and raced
them through the village.
When he got home, the horses
were sweaty and panting. Claude
never let him take the horses again.
            ~

My grandfather had a driver's license
but rarely used the car.
One afternoon he took my uncle
for a drive in the white Chev Impala.
When they got back, he swerved
quickly into the driveway.
At the last moment, realizing
there were no reins in his hands,
he stepped hard on the brakes, stopping
just before the bumper reached the barn.
            ~

These old stories glimmer and fade,
return years later, hardly changed at all.
Now I see my grandfather as an old
workhorse, who has just broken loose
from his pasture. He walks slowly up
Spring Brook Hill to a place
where the rugosa roses
are opening in the morning light.
How sweet they taste; how good
it feels to be unbridled at last.

THE CLOUDS

— for Katie and Amelia

Years ago, my daughter and I were in love with the
clouds. We sat at the picnic table as dusk came on. "Dad,"
she said, "where are the clouds going? To supper?" Yes,
my dear, to supper, to the final banquet of the light.
They'll sleep all night in the trees above the hill until the
day comes out again.

IV

Broken Psalms

BROKEN PSALM

– in memory of William Butler Yeats

All the cockles of my heart lay about me.
I knew this as I stood on the beach at Ballycastle,
looking at the shells along the shore that resembled
the chambers of an opened heart.

That night in Sligo, I walked across the stone bridge
to a tiny pub to hear music. One man played
the uilleann pipes. I was mesmerized.
On the way back to the hotel, two swans swam

on the dark river like pieces of light.
Near Castletown, on either side of the road,
fields of potatoes gleamed in the morning sun.
I half expected to see the ghost of Rose Eliza Kyle

working the rows, worrying the stalks from the earth.
I could feel the tubers swelling beneath the soil.
Somewhere I could hear a fiddle playing an old tune
that scratched the soul like the thorns of ancient roses.

This is my love, my earth, my broken psalm.
At Drumcliffe Churchyard I read Yeats's poem
over his grave: *"... the mountain grass
Cannot but keep the form*

Where the mountain hare has lain."
I heard the wind, and a woman's voice rising
in that wind. It was late spring. It was the beginning
of the new millennium, but I knew time kept no track

of my comings and goings, my risks and losses,
my secret conversations with the dead.
If these poems seem broken like fallen gravestones
then that's all right. In between the new leaves of the alders

Rose Eliza's double rose, a dusky pink, opens
its peppery scent. It opens once for me,
once for my love, and once for the world that lives
in the earth and the air and the sea.

THE VOICE

When I find something missing in the world, it's good to listen to the cadence of voices. One or two notes is enough. The first light of daybreak says nothing, and yet its persistent return is something the birds notice first.

Sometimes the dawn resembles a child who is just beginning to walk. There's a slight wobble that remains until everything comes into focus. A dream voice says, "If I can't walk there, I can always fly." It's a voice as calm and wise as the old Taoists, or the spruce that has clung to the edge of a cliff for five hundred years. It simply agreed to stay.

MOMENTS PRESSING UP FROM THE
OTHER WORLD

I remember a day in 1974, reading *The Secret Life of Plants* –
I realized that plants feel pleasure and pain, and maybe
the pleasure and pain of our existence as well.

I remember the trout diminishing in Cleveland Brook,
year after year, and the day I hung my fishing rod
in the rafters of the woodshed a final time.

I remember a yellow finch flailing in the dirt at the side
of the road; I picked him up, and he looked into my eyes,
shuddered, and died. I thought, *How many times*

will I look into the face of death before I die?
I remember the day my daughter found a small raccoon
lolling in the long autumn grass at Laverty Lake;

we gave him a peach, and he played with it between
his paws. When we went back the next day, he was gone.
A cold wind was blowing. Absence filled the air.

I remember as a child seeing a sandhill crane. Its wings
were so wide they seemed to touch both sides of the river.
When my grandfather died, I felt the distance that is inside

and outside at the same time. I remember counting pebbles
I'd gathered from a stream, three brown, two white,
and five a mottled grey – added up they numbered

the years of my life. I remember a tombstone
in the cemetery up the road – *Infant son of ...* chiselled
in the white marble. How big was his soul? And how far

did he travel, his soul-path as wide as the wings
of the sandhill crane? I remember a dream voice saying,
"How could your mother live like that for five years?"

But she did, until words left her and we talked
to each other with our eyes. As the days wore on
toward her dying, my wife said, "Her eyes

are as deep as whale eyes," and they were.
How could I forget my father's eyes that morning
when he died into something so profound

the landscape rang with grieving, his eyes
embers burning all that I cherished
from my childhood?

I was there when a soul went out from the body –
the same soul for everything, they say – each
as small as a grain of sand, only lighter.

THE BREAD OF THE DAY

On those days when words won't come to me
I wander around in the sunlight
and watch my small

granddaughter
running through the field, filled
with the wildness of the world.

I wonder about my mother. After she died,
could she hear me talking to her, grief
caught between my words like ashes?

I wonder if my father, after he died,
woke up as a small boy again
eating at his parents' table, taking inside

the bread of a day that will never end.
I wonder if there's something out there
larger than we are that holds our failures

and counts them, and feels
the gravity of our lives. I wonder
if there's something that catches

inside us, something
that makes us see that we
must dig deep to find the old wells

of compassion and love. I wonder
if there's something like prayer
moving through us.

HEAVEN

We all make our own kind
of heaven. My father always said,
"Mornings are the best."

I remember him
heading out the door
just after breakfast

and sunrise, his green cap
on his head, pruning shears and a small
saw in his hand to make

openings for the light.
Such a simple task, and yet
sometimes it seems that these

are the most important tasks of all.
Today my father's voice rose
through the river willows

as I walked outside,
not early, not late,
but just in time

to see him standing
exactly where I stood,
just in time

to catch one memory
still soaked with the dew
of early morning.

KEATS

When John Keats wrote about
the blue fields of heaven,
he wasn't speaking only
of the sky.

But what about those common
fields along back roads
where no one has lived
for generations, fields that cling

to a stubbornness
that defies alders,
pin cherries,
swamp maples?

The earth is always saying
goodbye to something:
a toad, a seed,
the footprints

of someone
who walked here
two hundred years ago.
John Keats said

Lift me up
as he died.
Did he find
some ordinary

silence, or
the blue fields
of heaven?
The earth gives us

her gold, even if it's only
the last old oak leaves
hanging on
in the autumn wind.

THE LIGHT THAT MOVES THROUGH
EVERYTHING

I want to write a poem
that brings things back to me again:
my granddaughter sitting in her wagon

surveying her kingdom of rocks and streams
and fallen leaves; my daughter sleeping on the floor
beside me as I worked; my father sitting in his chair

doing crossword puzzles and smoking his pipe
as he tallied the gains and losses in his life;
his father before him playing

"Will Your Anchor Hold" or "Jerusalem" as the snow
fell slow outside the window. I want to bring my friend
inside this poem, John Thompson talking

to my mother and father, his face so young
it startled me. I watched from the edge
of my dream, a man who had outlived them all.

I want to bring the animals I've loved and fed
to this poem; they wander away into a day
that will never end. I want to bring birds

fallen from branches, words tethered
which I now let go, as we all must let go
in the end. What is it that feeds us?

What in the world stays with us
after the contrails of our lives burn down
like a long summer dusk that lingers into the dark?

I hear words I spoke to my mother in her time of dying;
I hear old voices catching in the river willows,
but there's no one else here – or perhaps

it's the light inside everything that says,
"I move through all things equally, the loved and the lost,
and this is the measure you must draw from your days."

WANT

I want to meet that young man
I knew forty years ago
and tell him that I'm still writing poems;

that Robert Bly is ninety-three
and Donald Hall has just died;
I want to tell him that many

of the people he loved
are gone, or lost, but as you get
older you carry them inside you,

here, in your chest, like a sudden pang
or the first stirrings of desire or true love.
I want to tell him I still live

in the white house of memory;
it's filled with presence and absence,
although there are times when there's more presence

than absence, and the old days shine again.
I want to tell him it's October,
and the first yellow and gold leaves

are falling to the earth as they did for him,
leaves that resemble hands holding the invisible thread
between the heart and its desire.

I want to tell that young man that the fears
and doubts he felt back then
never completely leave – they fade

for a bit and return, often stronger than before.
I want to tell him that there are days
when I feel that every cell of my body

is a kind of womb that holds and protects
all the earthly hopes he had, and that nothing
really goes away, it just becomes something else.

I want to tell him what Hank Williams said
in a song he probably wouldn't have listened to
all those years ago, a song that is almost a poem.

Everyone needs an old song
to heal the heart, a song the colour blue
that is so lonesome

you can hear the sadness breaking open
to become a whippoorwill, a midnight
train, the sound of a falling star.

GOD'S EAR

I'd forgotten that my hands resemble
my mother's; they were made to play the piano
or lift a young child into my arms.

Sometimes I forget the music of my childhood,
but when I do, Spike Jones and his City Slickers
come back and sing to me again.

Sometimes I forget that the day
is pure, untouched by anything,
a snowy pasture filling with silence and light.

Sometimes I forget the locks and keys
to my imagination, but when I remember,
the new words open their wings and fly.

I've forgotten so many things, but I remember
how much I love you, and what I'll say when I find
my face close to the heavy webbing of God's ear.

THE OPEN DOOR

It was early autumn.
I sat in the porch
with one lamp only,
working on poems.

My wife
was singing in the kitchen.
My daughter played
in the next room.

The night was wild,
branches and leaves
tossed in heavy wind,
hitting the windows

like someone
from the other world
trying to find
their way back in.

It seemed to me
that the big white house
was a ship plowing
through the stars

and the night, carrying
a cargo
that was as secret
as human love itself.

It was a night of song
and leaves.
It was a night
when everyone

was happy
and in the right place.
Something silver
shone through the dark.

Whoever was trying
to get back in
found an open door
that night.

OLD SOCK

– for Laurie

Desire is no longer the small wooden boat
I loved as a child, floating down small ditches
swollen with spring rain;

desire is no longer the young girl
I loved in grade school, her long dark hair braided
and tied back in a bun.

I no longer feel the desire
of a ten-year-old boy riding his red bicycle
faster and faster, almost catching up with the wind.

When I say desire
the sound slips past my tongue, and my hands
reach out for something they will never hold.

What I desire is like waking up
in the middle of the night and seeing snow
fall and fall, with a three-quarter moon riding above it.

This hunger in my throat and my chest
is merely my longing for you, whom I've loved
for thirty-nine years. I don't expect it to change,

but I remember the wild look in your eyes
when I met you that said we could be whatever
we want, as long as we see our desire

reflected in each other's eyes.
Have I courted desire long enough?
Do I know what's coming around the next corner,

or what it means when someone
I've never met before speaks words
that are as clear to me as the old hymn book of love?

What is our anchor and what does it hold?
What is the boat that we board every morning
as the sun opens up like a jewel inside an old sock?

In the end it may be
that we desire what we must desire,
that it was born the moment we were born

and it depends on this body
growing older but not less lovely,
with all its scars and weeping places,

where grief comes to live for a while
but not forever. I give you this desire – take it
or leave it – it is part of me

as the earth
is part of the roots of every plant
and depends on them unconditionally.

AFTERWORD

This new collection, *Waiting For the Small Ship of Desire*, is a departure for me and contains some of the most personal poems I have written. I began the book during a dry period in my writing. One afternoon I thought, *Why don't I write what I'm thinking about when I'm unable to write poems?* So I did. Distinct moments and presences came back to find me: my young daughter sleeping on the floor beside me as I wrote; memories about my parents and grandparents; lines by John Keats, whom I read as a boy; and my old friends John Thompson and Robert Bly. I also wrote a series of poems based on dreams I had just before and during the time of my mother's death, which also was a new departure.

Those memories and presences began to gather like filings around a magnetic core, and I wrote intensely for twelve months. In fact, it seemed that the bulk of this raw material was almost completing itself, something I hadn't experienced for a very long time.

The final two sections of the book, "The Star's Way Home" and "Broken Psalms," deal with how accumulated memories and experiences shape our sense of place and home. The collection as a whole is a long meditation on life, love, and the changing face of desire as we grow older.

Allan Cooper

ACKNOWLEDGEMENTS

Some of these poems first appeared in *Arc, Eloizes, Salon* (the literary supplement of the *Telegraph-Journal*), and *The Forehead Review*.

The prose poems in "Two Glimpses" appeared in the *Best Canadian Poetry in English, 2010*, published by Tightrope Books.

This collection was created during the tenure of an Arts Grant A, artsnb. I thank artsnb for its continuing support of my work.

I wish to thank Laurie Armstrong Cooper, Leigh Faulkner, Thomas Hodd, Patrick McKinley, and Harry Thurston for helping me with this book.

I am indebted to J. P. Seaton and Jonathan Chaves for their work with the poems of Yuan Mei.

My translation of the poem "Planting Trees" by Yuan Mei quoted in the poem "Yuan Mei" first appeared in *The Deer is Thirsty for the Mountain Stream* (Owl's Head Press, 1992).

BOOKS BY ALLAN COOPER

Blood-Lines (Fiddlehead Poetry Books, 1979)

Hidden River Poems (Fiddlehead Poetry Books, 1982)

Bending the Branch (Percheron Press, 1983)

Poems Released on a Nuclear Wind (Pottersfield Press, 1987)

To an Unborn Child (Leaping Mountain Press, 1988)

The Pearl Inside the Body (Percheron Press, 1991)

Heaven of Small Moments (Broken Jaw Press, 1998)

Singing the Flowers Open (Gaspereau Press, 2001)

Gabriel's Wing (Gaspereau Press, 2004)

The Alma Elegies (Gaspereau Press, 2007)

Everything We've Loved Comes Back to Find Us
    (Gaspereau Press, 2017)

Toward the Country of Light (Pottersfield Press, 2018)